# Co$ting
## for
# Profit

A Professional's Guide
to Effective Costing

# By Frances Harder
3rd Edition

Author of "Fashion for Profit"

W9-BXQ-353

# Table of Contents

# Dedication

I dedicate this important little book, **Costing for Profit**, a accompanying book to Fashion For Profit to apparel manufacturers who are either in business, or about to begin the exciting and challenging adventure of apparel entrepreneurship. Being inspired and remaining creative while trying to realize a profit can be a daily challenge. I have written this little book with the intent of assisting manufactures and those wishing to open their own retail store to become more profitable in their business. Today's manufacturers represent the future of our industry and will ultimately be responsible for the economic success of our country's apparel industry. I request that it be a priority for everyone to find ways to support small businesses.

The key people that I would like to thank for helping with the important information needed to compile this book are: Henry Cherner, friend and partner, AIMS (Apparel Information Management System), for his help with content. We are all saddened by his early loss in the fall of 2017. Richard Stern for his advice and expertise. A special thanks to Josh Marron for his help in formatting and assisting with his graphic talents both Fashion For Profit 10th edition, Brand Building for Profit 3rd edition and Costing for Profit 3rd edition.

Also, to Nancy Spalding for her editing skills and industry expertise.

Special thanks to my friend Kathryn Hagen for the great book cover illustration for all my other recent new editions!

Special thanks to my husband, children and grandchildren! :)

# Preface

Frances Harder, in her words is, the "designer gone insane", who has fashion and the apparel industry in her blood! She studied fashion design in England and has enjoyed some exciting design positions in the world of fashion both within the United States, and internationally. She is the daughter of a clothing designer, and the granddaughter of a lace maker from Nottingham, England. Her uncle owned his own clothing manufacturing company in Nottingham, and her aunt had her own dress making business and retail store in Nottingham. Frances's father was a chemist of dye stuff for ICI in Northern England.

Frances has also been an educator and designer for over thirty years and has taught fashion at many prestigious colleges on both sides of the pond. She was able to call upon all of her talents in founding and developing the Fashion Business Incorporated (FBI), an educational non-profit, which provided business intelligence and business development for small apparel companies. The FBI closed after 19 years its 501c3 non-Profit doors in 2017 but with the help of her new team Frances then launched Fashion For Profit the new online platform that is a for profit entity. Commerce is beginning to realize that short term education is one of the most powerful armaments for their ultimate success. The new Fashion For Profit platform offers knowledge through online resources, consultants, freelance designers, International resources, seminars and customized training programs. (See more details about membership at the end of the book.)

Prior to founding the Fashion Business Incorporated in 1999 Frances was a full time Associate Professor at Otis College of Art in Los Angeles. As a result of her teaching and her own entrepreneurial experiences, Frances realized that there was a real need for business development information for creative designers, and decided to write a "how to" book Fashion For Profit, first edition 1998. The book is now in its tenth edition and has become the guide for anyone who wishes to start their own apparel company. It is also used widely by colleges and universities as a capstone class.

*Frances's mantra is "sharing knowledge with others will ultimately benefit us all".*

# Introduction

Costing For Profit is a comprehensive guide that will help you analyze the preparation of a cost sheet correctly, which will ultimately determine a profitable company. The cost sheet provides critical information for every department involved in the process of producing the finished garment, from design through the production cycle, to distribution of the finished products being shipped to your customer.

The results of proper cost sheet preparation provide a company with essential analytical information for Gross Profit auditing controls. The total of all costs related to the production of the products is called COST OF GOODS SOLD referred to in the industry as COGS.

The cumulative information for all styles will be reflected in your Financial Statement. The difference between the Cost of Goods Sold and the Wholesale Price of the products being offered to the retail market is the Gross Profit.

The percentage between the Cost of Goods Sold and the Wholesale Price reflected in the cumulative sales each season and each year is your profit Margin.

Thus if the Wholesale price of the Garment is $50.00

The Cost of Goods Sold is $25.00

The difference of $25.00 is the Gross Profit

The Gross Profit is 50%.

The gross profit of $25.00 must also provide the funds to pay the company's daily overheads, plus sales representative's commission. This may sound simple but one missed cost or miscalculation can be devastating to your business.

Apparel manufacturers tend to develop or adapt their own way of calculating cost to arrive at their final wholesale price. Some very successful companies have fine-tuned their costing department to make the company profitable. Others unfortunately, unwittingly consider it more important to concentrate on design and realize too late that, although it seems more rewarding to design beautiful clothes. The "Business of Fashion" is a business, and ultimately must be about effective costing in order to make a profit.

Because of the many differences used within the industry in calculating their wholesale selling price, I have outlined a number of scenarios in this important little book, which will show a number of ways to calculate your costs to determine your selling price and still realize a profit. Whichever method a company should develop to cost their garments, the end result must result in a profitable margin at the end of the season.

# Co$ting for Profit

# Costing For Profit

Understanding the many components involved in costing a garment correctly will be the key to your company's success.

There are different ways of calculating your wholesale selling price.

Whichever method you choose, your final calculations must result in a profit!

One small miscalculation or a forgotten cost will be devastating to your profit margins, and ultimately undermine the survival of your business.

Small creative companies are often preoccupied with designing, and underestimate the importance of costing and their **actual** overheads.

Their costs are not always correctly detailed until after market, and the orders are in. This can be detrimental to the profitability of a company.

Educate yourself to realize **ALL** cost involved in manufacturing your line and what you will need to operate your business.

**Costing For Profit** will help you to realize your dream of being a successful designer and the owner of a profitable business.

# Why does a dress cost $300 at Niemans and $29.99 at Target?

**What contributes to the final selling price of a garment?**

- $ Complexity of the design
- $ Status of the label or brand
- $ Produced overseas or domestically
- $ Fabric cost
- $ Retailer store from which the dress is purchased

**To the consumer the cost of clothing is often a perceived value**

# $tep One!

So where do we begin to cost a garment and ultimately realize a profit?

Planning is the key to making your dreams a reality!

# Market Research is Essential

**To determine your price bracket or market niche, ask these questions:**

$ Who is your target market: age group, social economic income group?

$ What location: statewide, nationwide or global reach?

$ Why would they buy your product?

$ Does your product fill a niche?

$ Is there a need for your product?

$ Which stores would buy your product?

$ Which other brands are your competition?

# After Market Research

**What would be the selling price range for your product?**

$ To cost too high could mean no orders

$ To charge too little could result in no profits, or even worse, losses

$ Miscalculation can be devastating to your profit margins, and could determine whether or not your start-up business can survive

$ Important to retain quality of styling and construction within the set price structure

**Informed correct costing will be the key to your company's success**

# Keep Your Market Analysis Updated

The apparel business is a global industry that is constantly changing. To eliminate risk it is important to have as many facts as possible. Stay on course and consistently monitor your business and THE business as this will influence your costs.

Whether manufacturing domestically or internationally with global distribution, every world variable will have some effect on your costs.

$ Constantly shop stores both locally and globally

$ Check your demographics to make sure it is not changing

$ Don't forget your target market

# Formal Business and Financial Plan

$ Make sure that your business plan is updated

$ Has your executive structure changed?

$ How are you financed?

$ Do you have a financial plan for when the BIG orders are written?

$ Plan to grow using the stair steps growth principal - one step at a time. Planning a steady growth will get you there

$ To grow too fast could be a short lived exciting experience

$ Not having time to find the right people to help grow your company could jeopardize your success

A sales rep does not want to write orders if you don't have the funds to deliver!

# Branding Process

**Creating a brand or logo should be the ultimate goal for any garment manufacturer.**

$ The consumer will often pay more for a branded label rather than for a non branded label

$ Eventually licensing a successful brand will create a passive cash flow

$ In other words consumers and other types of product manufacturers will pay you money to advertise your product!!

$ However, you first have to pay out a lot of money to market your own image and brand

$ Advertising requires big bucks, unless you can get on Oprah!!

$ Should you receive free PR or pay for it yourself, make sure you are capable of meeting the demand

$ Have you planned your production capacity and your financing capabilities to match the demand?

It should be noted that for some branded companies there is an optimal level of growth, which they should not exceed. Without the infrastructure in place to deal with rapid growth, it could lead a company to failure.

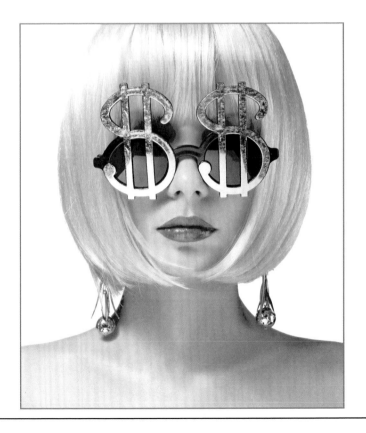

# Trade Mark Licensing

**First you must trademark your logo and your company's name**

$ It is important to protect your company's image and the integrity of your label

$ If you have a great idea for a new product seek the advice of an expert

$ Trademark licensing should be done by an attorney who understands the apparel industry

$ Are you trade marking your logo in one State or across the US?

$ How will you handle the Global reach?

$ In which other countries do you plan on selling your product?

$ How will you protect your product should you decide to sell internationally?

$ The costs involved in trade marking a brand internationally is very expensive

# $tep Two!

## Determining Price Point

**Your Price Point will usually be determined by your selling price at retail.**

# Price Range

**You must stay within the chosen price range**

$ Identify who is your target market & what they will be willing to pay

$ Identify your competition & their price points

$ What is your wholesale and retail price range that your garments should fit into? Then calculate backwards to your costing

$ Make sure that the quality and styling is retained for your market niche

$ Your manufacturing cost + profit. This should calculate to the appropriate profit margin necessary to make a PROFIT!

$ Remember that if your selling price is too high you will cost yourself out of the chosen market

$ If your margins are too low, you are in danger of not making a profit

• **Important to keep in control!**

# Cost

**COST IS THE ONLY VARIABLE WHICH CAN BE CONTROLLED BY YOU!**

**$  Price = Cost + Profit**

$  Understanding the key elements when costing will assure your gross & net profit margin

$  Check your math: Can your garments stand the retailer mark-up of 120% (to them 54% margin) and still have a customer demand for your product? Example:

    Your wholesale price:    $50.00
    Retailer markup (120%):  $60.00
    Retail selling price:     $110.00

Retailer margin: $\dfrac{60}{110} x100 = 54\%$

$  You must consistently deliver three things:

    **$  Price**

    **$  Quality**

    **$  On-Time Deliveries**

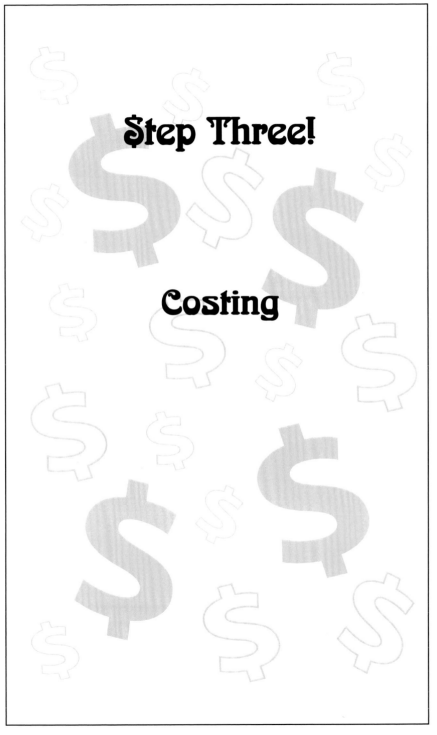

# $tep Three!

# Costing

# Three stages of costing

1. **"Actual cost" of production:** This is the cost to produce the garment and is determined by the fabric, design and production, which can only be reduced by modifying or changing the garment. If producing overseas, this is your landed cost (including freight and duty) or COGS.

2. **Cost plus your markup percentage:** Your mark-up will be determined by a couple of factors: How many units you need to manufacture in order to cover your overhead to realize a profit, and what your market niche will bear. This should be laid out in your business plan and followed.

3. **Retail-selling price:** Having a realistic understanding of the price structure of the market place will help when determining the final cost. Retailers profit margin is usually around a 54% margin.

The final retail price must always be considered when choosing fabric, trims and styling your line. *Don't be tempted to love that fabric from Italy too much without adjusting and simplifying your styling!*

# Profit Margin

**Your PROFIT MARGIN is PRE-DETERMINED BY YOU & SHOULD NOT BE UNDERCUT**

$ If you have a large, potential order from a department store, and they want you to reduce your profit margin, do your math and make sure it is possible to reduce your profit margin and still make a profit

$ Just because you get a large order, it is not necessarily in your company's best interest

$ Take the time to read all sales documents and agreements

$ **You must rework your numbers before you accept orders if there are any requests for discounts!**

$ **If you do receive a large order, check with your contractor to see if they will discount their cost**

$ **However, if you don't get the agreed to orders that your contractor requires for his production run; DON'T TAKE THE ORDER!**

# Costs of Handling

**Smaller orders from specialty stores require more handling.**

$ Results in more hands on time to pick and pack these smaller shipments

$ Increases hourly time needed for workers to complete this process

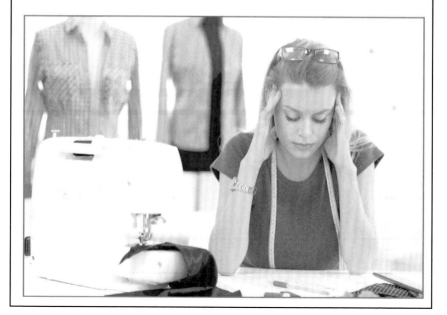

# Importance of Accurate Costing

**Underestimating or guessing costs can be disastrous to your long term success.**

Incorrect costing can result in losses & eventually bankruptcy for a company.

$ Costing should be done before any orders are written

$ Projecting the size of your production will effect your costing

$ Know your minimum numbers for each style. Don't be tempted to sell ones & twos!!

$ Never guess: Cutting costs, labor costs, trims or yardage!

$ Rework your cost sheets if a style is carried over to a second season

# Major Costs

## Fabric

## Trims

## Labor

$ The bigger the order, usually unit prices decrease

$ Important to project the amount of goods you need to sell so as to cost realistically. *This is often hard, but **must** be planned for*

$ You may produce domestically, or off-shore; these are major factors in determining the cost of your goods sold

$ If producing off-shore and paying by letters of credit or purchase order financing, be certain to include your financing costs

$ If borrowing money from a lender, asset based financing or using credit cards, you must be certain to include the financing or interest costs

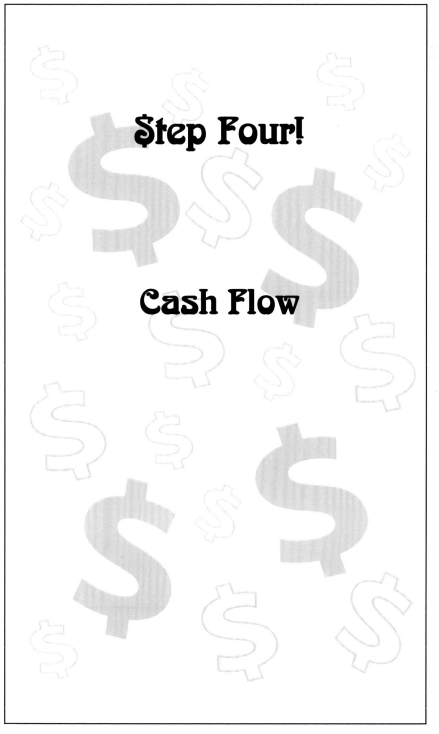

# $tep Four!

# Cash Flow

# Cash Flow is Key!

**Identify potential sources of funding before the need arises.**

$ It is critical for you to understand your financial plan and your cash flow needs

$ Turning away orders can be hard, but if the funds are not available to produce your orders you may have no alternative

$ Investigate all funding options before going to market

$ It is most important to plan and retain control of your business!

$ Even with the best of plans, costs are always higher than expected

# Working capital has a direct impact on your cash flow

**Cash flow is the name of the game for all business owners, a good understanding of working capital is imperative to make any venture successful and profitable.**

Know when your invoices are expected to be paid, then you will know when to plan on paying your vendors. However, prepare for late payers.

Try and get your buyers to pay on their credit card. This type of payment is normal practice for small specialty stores. They get the credit card points or mileage and you get paid the day you ship them their goods. This **REALLY** helps your cash flow problems and is a very good reason to stay loyal to your small stores.

**Important to note: department stores are a whole different story. You should not sell to them until you are prepared and able to work with them!**

**Department stores rarely pay on time and they will often charge back to you for reasonable and unreasonable infractions, which they claim you have made.**

# Building Your Trade Credit

It is important to ask all your vendors, if they will give you time to pay them. It may take a couple of orders before they agree to this, but begin by asking for a 7 days grace period to pay your invoice. As they build trust in your commitment to pay them, ask for more time.

If you get rejected for the full amount, try and bargain with half now and the other half in 10 days.

Even if you don't need the credit in the beginning ask for it anyway.  As your company grows, the time will come when you will need that extra time to pay your vendors. The faster your company grows with more orders, the more money you will need to fulfill them.

The credit your vendors extend to you will be built on them taking the financial risk. It will depend on your relationship with them. So be nice!

# Seasonal Selling

**Saving for a rainy day.**

$ It is important to make as much money as possible during the selling months, and calculate your break even financial needs in the off seasons

$ If your sales are not always on the rise, you will need to calculate your monthly overheads to meet the downtime in your sales cycle

$ How many sales do you need to cover overheads? Remember this amount will need to be increased as your sales rise

$ How easy will it be if sales go down to meet the monthly overheads?

# Final Selling Price

**The final selling price of a garment is a product of total cost of goods sold** (If produced overseas, landed cost = finished product, plus freight, plus duty, plus financing cost if using PO, or an LC, plus currency conversion if paying in a foreign currency).

$ Plus the markup needed to reach your desired profit margins

$ Take all this into account, and the retail markup. Does this allow you to sell your product competitively?

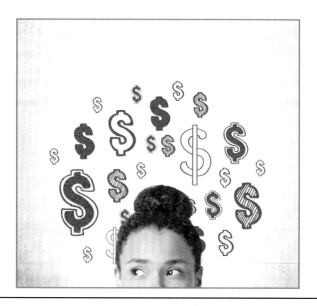

# Fixed Costs

**Fixed Costs are expenses that a business always has. It is important to be aware of them and to keep a track of all fixed costs.**

$   Staff – full time and part time

$   Design development  - (too often over looked), sample fabric, first patterns, samples, production patterns, quality control, bookkeeping and shipping

$   Overhead costs or fixed costs should not be forgotten, including rent, electricity, payroll etc.

$   Keep an eye on these expenses when figuring your markups

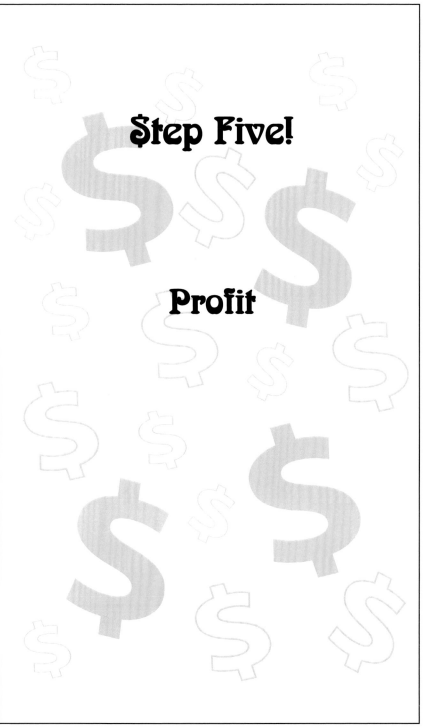

Step Five!

Profit

# Examples of Costing

**The following will detail different ways to calculate your costs and arrive at a net profit**

$ The preferred method: Gross profit less overheads, sales expenses and discounts will give you your true net profit

$ Whichever method you choose to use, the trick is to be aware of all costs and to recost at every level to check for any miscalculations, hidden, or forgotten costs

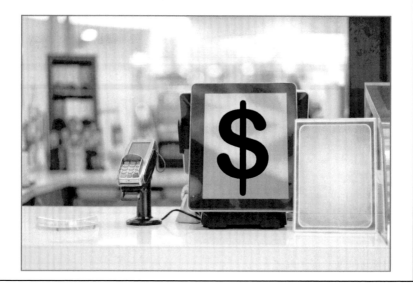

# Keystone Costing

**Keystoning is a simplified costing method, which is often used but not always fully understood**

$ **Twice your cost, (or is it?)**

$ Are all your overhead expenses calculated or considered into your costing method?

$ Will this really give you a 100% mark-up?

$ **Example:** If your basic cost is $20, you will sell your garment for $40 = **100% mark-up**

$ You go back from the $40 to your cost of $20 , that will equal a **50% gross profit margin**

$ **Important! The gross profit is the foundation to calculate your net profit**

# Example of Keystone Costs
## Without subtracting overhead costs

## Fabric Costs

A blouse takes two yards of fabric

| | |
|---|---|
| 2 yards @ $4 .00 per yard | $8.00 |
| Freight for fabric @ 15 cents per yard | $0.30 |
| Total Fabric cost | $8.30 |

## Miscellaneous Costs

| | |
|---|---|
| Block Fusing | $0.20 |
| 7 Buttons @ 2 cents each | $0.14 |
| 1 Label@ 2 cents each | $0.02 |
| Miscellaneous costs | $0.36 |

## Labor Charges

| | |
|---|---|
| Cutting | $1.50 |
| Sewing & Labor | $5.00 |
| Marking & grading | $1.00 |
| Total Labor cost | $7.50 |

| | |
|---|---|
| **Your Total cost** | **$16.16** |
| **Keystone: 100% Mark-up** | **$16.16** |
| **Total  Wholesale Price** | **$32.32** |

(You may round out your wholesale price)

# Keystone Gross Profit
## Without subtracting Overhead costs

$   Keystone: 100% mark-up $16.16

$   Total wholesale price $32.32

$   100% markup = 50% gross profit

$   This calculation does not consider your overhead expenses including: rent, administrative and sales expenses

$   These must be deducted from your gross profit to get to your net profit

**Important: Smaller manufacturers should aim for at least a 55% to 65% gross profit margin, because of the small amount of units manufactured.**

# Ret Profit Cost Calculations
## Without subtracting overhead cost

| | |
|---|---|
| Wholesale Price | $32.32 |
| Subtract Cost of Goods Sold (COGS) | $16.16 |
| Gross Profit | $16.16 |

**Net Profit Calculation**

| | |
|---|---|
| Wholesale Price | |
| Your selling price | $32.32 |
| Subtract Sales commission 10% | $3.23 |
| After commission | $29.09 |
| Subtract Actual Cost of Garment | $16.16 |
| Net Profit                **Total** | $12.93 |
| without subtracting overheads | |

# Net Profit is your tax base

# Net Profit Margin Calculations
## Without subtracting overheads

Divide the Net Profit by the wholesale price, then multiply by 100

$$\frac{\$12.93}{\$32.32} x100 = 40\%$$

**40% is your Net Profit Margin**

(Without including overheads or discounts allowable)

# Discounts Allowable for Early Payments

**Buyers will often ask for a discount on their orders if they agree to make payment to you within 30 days**

$ Discounts vary but normally fall into the 8% to 10%

$ Even if they don't intend to pay within 30 days they will often expect these discounts

$ It can take between 60 to 90 days to receive payment from major department stores

$ This should be carefully monitored as it will affect your cash flow

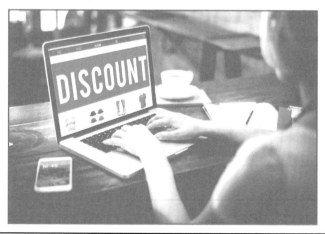

# Net Profit Cost Calculations
## With discounts included but no overhead costs

| | |
|---|---|
| Wholesale Price | $32.32 |
| Subtract Cost of Goods Sold (COGS) | $16.16 |
| **Gross Profit margin** | **$16.16** |

**Net Profit Calculation**

| | |
|---|---|
| Wholesale Price | $32.32 |
| Subtract Discounts allowable 10% | $3.23 |
| **Your new selling price** | **$29.09** |
| Subtract Sales commission 10% | $2.90 |
| After discounts and commission | $26.19 |
| | |
| Subtract Actual Cost of Garment | $16.16 |
| Net Profit **Total** | **$10.03** |
| without including overhead costs | |

## Net Profit is your taxable base

# Net Profit Margin Calculations
### With discounts included but no overhead costs

Divide the Net Profit by the wholesale price, then multiply by 100

$$\frac{\$10.03}{\$32.32} x100 = 31\%$$

**31% is your Net Profit Margin
(Without overhead costs)**

# Should You Add Overheads in Your Costs?

**Is it important to list ALL expenses in a cost sheet?**

$ Often, this method can cost a company out of the market, as the final selling cost will calculate too high!

$ **However, it is interesting to compare the different methods – so we will show you!**

$ In calculating your gross profit margin, do not include any expenses that are not directly related to the cost of the finished goods

$ Overhead costs are not usually included in gross profit margin calculations

$ If you include your overhead costs in your cost sheet, they should be calculated on the number of units you plan on selling

# Example of Keystone Costs
### Including overhead

## Fabric Costs

A blouse takes two yards of fabric

| | |
|---|---:|
| 2 yards @ $4 .00 per yard | $8.00 |
| Freight for fabric @ 15 cents per yard | $0.30 |
| Total Fabric cost | $8.30 |

## Miscellaneous Costs

| | |
|---|---:|
| Block Fusing | $0.20 |
| 7 Buttons @ 2 cents each | $0.14 |
| 1 Label@ 2 cents each | $0.02 |
| Miscellaneous costs | $0.36 |

## Labor Charges

| | |
|---|---:|
| Cutting | $1.50 |
| Sewing & Labor | $5.00 |
| Marking & grading | $1.00 |
| Total Labor cost | $7.50 |

## Overhead (Calculated on units produced)

| | |
|---|---:|
| | $1.50 |
| Your Total cost | $17.66 |
| Keystone: 100% Mark-up | $17.66 |
| **Total  Wholesale Price** | $35.32 |

(You may round out your wholesale price)

# Keystone Gross Profit Calculations

## Including overheads

Keystone: 100% mark-up            $17.66

Total wholesale price              $35.32

**100% markup = 50% gross profit**

**This calculation considers your overhead expenses: Administration, rent, cars...**

# Net Profit Calculations
## Including overheads & discounts

| | |
|---|---:|
| Wholesale Price | $35.32 |
| Subtract Cost of Goods Sold (COGS) | $17.66 |
| Gross Profit margin | $17.66 |

**Net Profit Calculation**

| | |
|---|---:|
| Wholesale Price | $35.32 |
| Subtract Discounts allowable 10% | $3.53 |
| **Your new selling price** | **$31.79** |
| Subtract Sales commission 10% | $3.18 |
| After commission is paid | $28.61 |
| Subtract Actual Cost of Garment | $17.66 |
| **Net Profit**                      **Total** | **$10.95** |

## Net Profit is your taxable base

# Net Profit Margin
## Including Overheads & Discounts

Divide the Net Profit by the wholesale selling price and then multiply by 100.

$$\frac{\$10.95}{\$35.32} \, x100 = 31\%$$

**31% is your Net Profit Margin**

# Profit Comparisons
## With or without Overheads

Whichever costing method you choose, the bottom line will be the real profit your company will ultimately take to the bank

A profit can only be realized when you fully understand the total components that need to be considered when calculating your net profit margin.

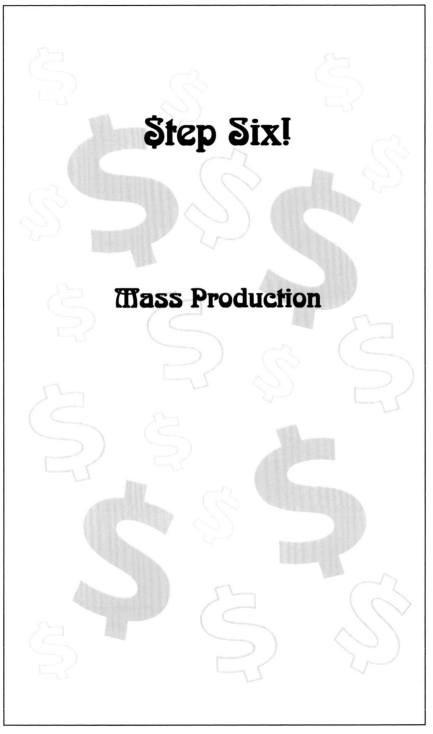

# $tep $ix!

## Mass Production

# Mass Production

"Mass" produced clothing can allow for a smaller mark-up due to the large quantities produced at one time.

For the most part mass produced clothing is produced off-shore.

Because of the lower cost of off-shore workers wages, it is difficult for US manufacturers to remain competitive.

Domestic contractors normally work with a 30% profit margin.

# Off-Shore Production

**Deciding to produce your goods off-shore will affect your wholesale selling price. However, before venturing abroad it is very important to answer these questions to fully understand the advantages and the disadvantages of taking this route.**

$ The question is why go off-shore?

$ What can off-shore versus domestic production offer?

$ When first thinking of taking production off-shore it will be important to test the system, and not put all your eggs into one basket

$ Begin with a 80/20 split. Diversify your production.

$ Keep 80% here, and test with 20% for first time off-shore production

$ Where do you go to find the right reliable resources?

$ How will your quality control be monitored?

$ Will you need to find an agent to represent your company and check your production?

$ How will you obtain lines of credit?

$ What is a Letter of Credit and how much will it cost?

$ How much Duty will there be on your imported goods, and how much will you pay? Duties vary depending on where the goods are produced

$ How will Quotas effect my production off shore?

$ How will currency charges and conversions costs add to your costs?

$ Will you still be able to meet delivery dates?

$ How much extra time will you need to allow for off-shore production?

$ How much should you allow for shipping costs?

These are reasons why many smaller companies produce only domestically where they can better control their quality, production and delivery times.

# Know Your Timelines

If you are investigating off-shore sourcing it will be important to understand the lead time. If your production is domestic and you are in the contemporary market then timing will be everything. Look at your delivery timeframe and know where your offshore production cycle is at all times.

**Once you find an off-shore source, what happens next?**

$ Do they need to purchase supplies, or do they already have them?

$ Do they make the goods, or have to send somewhere else?

$ How do they deal with their sub-contractors?

**It is very important to understand how long it's going to take to get the goods here and where they are at all times; from fabrication to production, to shipping.**

**It's a big mistake to underestimate the time line. If your shipment is late this will result in more dilution and cancelled orders.**

# Letters of Credit

$ It will be important to get a full understanding of how to open letters of credit

$ Talk with your bank and your factor. Some Asian companies will give credit much sooner than they used to

$ As with all aspects of running a successful business, it will be important to build reliable relationships

# $tep $even!

## Custom Made Clothing

## &

## Couture Costing

# Custom Made Clothing
# &
# Couture Costing

When costing a couture garment it is important to establish an hourly rate for the creator of these one of a kind garments.

One of a kind, couture, or sometimes referred to as wearable art, has nothing in common with manufactured clothing, as the costing must be calculated by the hours of work entailed in creating **one** finished garment.

If the custom-made piece has been commissioned, ask for a fifty percent up-front deposit and the other half on completion.

To guarantee payment upon completion, finished pieces may be shipped either COD cashier's check, or pro forma. (COD should only be agreed to with established vendors).

Important to have in writing and signed by your customer before commencing work, that any changes made to the design by your customer will incur an extra charge.

# $tep Eight!

## Private Label

# Private Label

**If commissioned to manufacture for a private label or for a branded logo, or for any special orders with embroidery, (example to manufacturer for Disney) it is important to require a 50% deposit up front. The remaining 50% is payable upon completion.**

*The reason for this requirement is that it would be impossible to sell the branded product should you not get paid and are left with the product.*

If commissioned to manufacturer private label for a specialty store your payment would be invoiced using the normal method.

# $tep Nine!

## Preparing a Cost Sheet

# Filling in a Cost Sheet

**Filling in the cost sheets yourself will be an invaluable lesson, and will teach you the true meaning of costing.**

There will be times that an adjustment will need to be made to the final gross margins to keep garments in the correct price range.

$ Only you can make this important decision!

$ Can the selling price be lowered?

**Be certain you can afford to adjust your wholesale selling price DOWN!**

# The following should be included or considered into a cost sheet

$ Date

$ Style number and design number (name if applicable)

$ Fabric mill – Cost per yard

$ Fabric yields, (include fabric shipping costs)

$ Linings

$ Trim cost, including fusing

$ Cutting

$ Labor & sewing

$ Swatch of the fabrics, trims

$ Send out information e.g. fusing, pleating, embroidery, printing, etc.

$ Packaging

$ Mark-up percentage: Which should consider: *Overhead costs, fixed costs, operational costs, sales Representative percentage, tradeshow expenses, and chargebacks. discounts or markdowns must be taken into account when calculation your final mark-up percentage, (not forgotten when selling to department stores)*

$ Wholesale price

$ Gross profit calculations

$ Net profit calculations

# Calculate Your Fixed Cost

Office staff salaries – More economic to employ part-time staff or hourly paid workers.

Full time salaries with benefits can add another 30 cents per hour on the dollar paid.

$  Rent – Contract out as much as possible in order to keep your overheads down and your office space rental as low as possible

$  Utilities etc

$  Lease rather than buy.  Monthly payments may be easier to figure into accounting rather than a large cash outlay if there is a cash crunch

A realistic percentage for fixed overheads should be around 5% - 7% of wholesale price.  If you have a 30% gross profit margin, and your fixed expenses are 10% of your net sales, this will undermine your profit. If that is the case, try to reduce your fixed expenses.

# Operational Costs

**Product development** – is an operational cost but only when developing new designs.

Design departments should be monitored closely for excessive expenditure:

How many samples produced per season?

**The average cost to develop one sample is approximately $500; fabric, first patterns, cutting, sewing, fitting and adjusting…**

Use computer programs to render your first designs. Scan your fabrics then drape virtually for your design development and for finished styles.

# Variable Costs

## Actual costs of product

$ Fabric

$ Trims

$ Labor

$ Size of cuts

*Agreeing to produce smaller lots can be costly and erode your profits.*

# Sales Representatives Percentages, Expenses and Discounts

**The percentage allowed your sales representative for sales commission plus showroom and tradeshow expenses should be considered into your costs.**

$ Also - Terms of Sales influencing the cost. Discounts for prompt payment by the store are often asked for by the buyers

$ Calculate the percentage of allowable discounts you can afford

$ The commission paid to your sales representatives is based on the final agreed to selling price (after allowable discounts) and the actual units shipped to the store

$ Showroom participation fees and trade show expenses should also be considered, as these can be very costly

$ *Better to pay a higher percentage to your sales rep than pay a fixed monthly showroom participation fee*

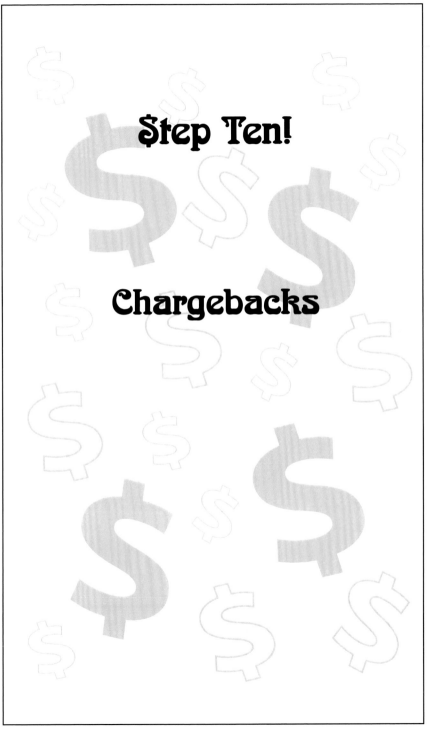

# $tep Ten!

# Chargebacks

# Chargebacks Destroy Your Profits

**Chargebacks undermine your gross profits and should be carefully monitored. Keep a close watch in the areas where they are most prevalent:**

$ Is it a problem with shipping, labeling, hangers, packaging or out of specifications?

$ Is it quality control, damages, or are there sizing issues?

$ Is it late shipments?

$ If you are selling to department stores it is usual to add between 12% and 15% to the cost sheet for the inevitable discounts and charge-backs. If you sell to specialty stores, the percentage should be around 6 to 8 percent

# Other Chargeback & Markdown Costs from Major Department Stores

$ Too few garments selling at full price – Retailer makes you share in the losses from discounted sales

$ Charges for advertising or promoting the product in store flyers and newspaper advertisements

$ Department stores will charge larger manufacturers rent to have their line displayed in a high traffic area within the store

*Remember! Markdown money or store credit adds to the manufacturer's variable costs.*

# Dilution of Profit

**This is the difference between what you invoice the retailer (customer) and what you get paid from your customer.**

**Example:**

$ Non-paying customers

$ Chargeback

$ Returns

$ Store discounts

$ Late shipment

$ Damaged goods

$ Purchase order (P.O.) violations

Generally the more expensive the product, the higher the percentage of dilution of sales. Customer returns are higher because of the pricing structure and should be an added cost consideration.

# Shipping Dates

$ It is better to ship at the beginning of the shipping window

$ This will allow for reorders and your goods to get onto the store floor for a longer period of time, which means they have a longer sell through time

$ Shipping at the end of your delivery window means that the goods aren't on the floor for that long, and they may be marked down sooner because of new goods arriving

$ Make sure that all separates are shipped together, (matching tops to bottoms)

$ Should your production not go as planned and you have a problem with related separates which you cannot ship together, then contact the buyer and inform them of any delivery problems

**It is crucial to control all parts of your production.**

# Retailer's Mark-up

**Retailers buy your product at a wholesale price, then add their overhead costs plus profits: between 100% to 125% to get the retail selling price.**

$ Retailers normally pay for any shipping charges

$ They will have requirements as to the shipping instructions and packaging details. It is important to understand your exact responsibilities for shipments and any hidden costs?

$ Anticipate your customer's demands and include them when considering your costs!

$ Do not let the retailers dictate their price, unless you know your profit margin can bear their asking price. It is important to protect your profit margin, and stay in control of your product costs

$ Ask your sales reps NOT to agree to store discounts without your approval

# Retailers Selling Price

It is important to establish a suggested retail selling price with your retailers.

If a retailer decides to mark up too high your line may not sell.

Your sales rep and/or yourself should inquire weekly with your accounts as to how your line is **"selling through"**.

This will provide you with important information as to which designs are selling, and which are your best sellers.

The best-selling items can be carried over to your next season's line.

The styles that are not selling should be analyzed as to the problem: fabric, fit, styling, or maybe you were ahead of the game with trend forecasting?

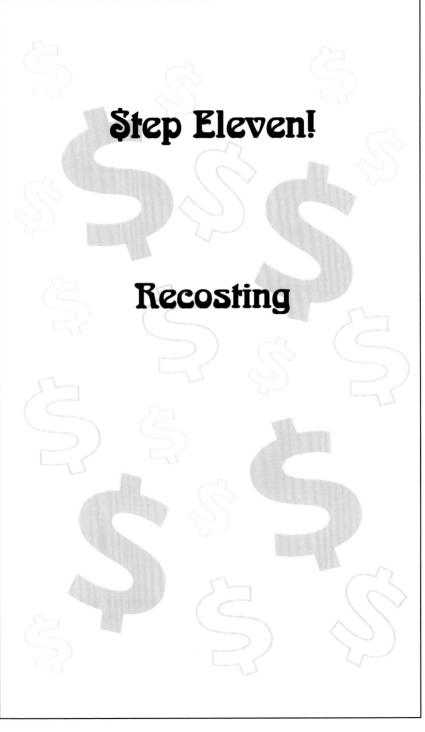

# $tep Eleven!

# Recosting

# Importance of Recosting

**Recost every new style, for every new season, and remember to rework the cost sheet.**

$ Beware of using the same cost sheet when changing fabrication, even if using the same style

$ There could be hidden costs that you are unaware of when changing the fabrication, such as differences in the fabric cost, the fabric width, the marker, production, finishing, pressing, etc

# Financing Your Line

**Depending on your funding it may be wise to start with small orders that you can self-finance so that when mistakes are made it will not be too financially and emotionally devastating to the company.**

$   You will learn by your mistakes

$   The secret to costing and financial success is understanding how to plan your company's growth

$   Finding financing for large orders when just starting a company will be difficult unless you have:

> $   Your own savings
>
> $   Family or friends as investors
>
> $   Line of credit
>
> $   Collateral

*Don't use credit cards, the interest rates are too high!*

# Factoring Orders or Using your assets to grow your business

**It is nearly impossible to factor a new business without a proven track record.**

$ A company needs to show experience and a profit

$ It is very difficult to get a 1st line of credit from traditional factoring

$ A company will need at least $500,000 in annual orders before a factor (first line of credit) or refactor (second line of credit) will agree to loan you money against your receivables

$ It helps to have orders from reputable stores

$ Begin early to build relationships with factors

$ Remember, factors take the risk and so they have to be cautious with their money

$ **You must retain a good credit rating!**

# How a Factor Can Help your Business

$ A factor will advance funds against your receivables (written orders) or against your collateral

$ Why factor? A factor can assist your company with cash flow problems and help solve financial burden

$ The day you ship you will receive 70% to 80% of invoice orders. You pay interest to the factor, (usually 2% above prime), plus a fee, until the invoice is paid by the store to the factor

$ Factors also check stores credit plus take the financial risk

$ They collect the money owed and then pay you the other 20% to 30% less fees

# Purchase Order Financing

**Is it a financial liability or a financial asset to your company?**

P.O. financing can be risky and therefore you must understand how to make it work for your company's cash flow crunch.

Money is loaned against your written orders to help with your upfront production costs; fabric, sewing, etc.

However, it is a very expensive way to borrow money and you must calculate this into your costs.

You will be borrowing and paying interest on the loan for at least two to three months before you are able to repay.

Can you afford this type of loan? It is important to factor the fees plus interest into your costs.

# Understand Delivery Dates

**Many design driven companies become enamored of their own designs and are convinced that the market will fall in love with their product. They often stock up without any regard to orders or to the financial downside. The goods inevitably end up discounted and consequently, there will be heavy losses to account.**

Caution is advised when speculating sales and asking for any kind of financial backing.

$ You should be 80% sold before arranging for any financing

$ **Not 20% and speculating 80%!**

$ This will result in inventory build up

**Important to build inventory on orders written, not on speculation! Management of inventory is key!**

# Understand Delivery Dates

**Late deliveries will result in cancelled orders or chargebacks, so it is important to know your delivery dates, which will reflect on your production dates.**

$ If March 30th, April 30th and May 30th are delivery dates, then you must work out your production dates with your contractor to avoid missing shipping deadlines

$ Get delivery dates in a written contract with your contractor

*Stick to your drop dead dates!*

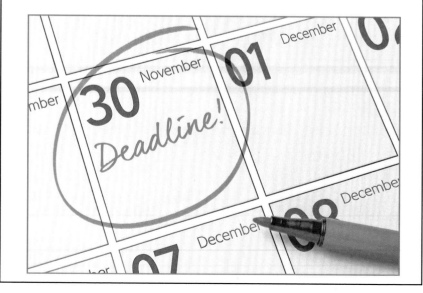

# $tep Twelve!

## Garment Costing for Success

## 10 Point Checklist for Profitable Results

# 1. Development Cost

Whatever type of garment you manufacture there is always development. These are known as hidden costs and should not be ignored.

Design room, sample room & product development cost can be top heavy. It is very important to control these cost as they are too often over looked.

Track these expenses by the season; number of samples produced, amount of sample yardage, and how many times a sample is made before it is accepted in the line.

# 2. First Sample or Prototype Cost

Check the number of times the average sample is made before the final garment is approved.

Samples produced should be controlled. Contractors charge approximately three times the cost of final production cost for sampling.

Typically a design driven contemporary company is higher-end and should cost for higher margins. However, they also tend to design and sample far too many, which results in too many SKU's.

Utilize computer software programs to help with product development costs, fabric rendering for color and style choices.

*The average cost of one sample is around $500 to develop the pattern, fabric, cut, sew, fit, and cost.*

# 3. Fabric Cost for Sampling

Fabric used for samples can add up. Keep a record of this part of development. You may be surprised at the amount of sample yardage ordered and not used.

*All those beautiful Italian fabrics at textile shows can often be too tempting for creative designers!*

# 4. Pattern Development Costs

*Experienced patternmakers can save a manufacturer money. Make sure you pay them for their experience, it will save you money in the long run!*

Pattern making can be more costly than realized. Keep an account of this part of your business expenses.

# 5. Yield of Fabric Costs

Your fabric expense may be 40% to 50% of the direct cost of the garment. Making sure that you are not wasting fabric and that your markers are good and tight is going to affect the overall profitability of your business.

*Employing an experienced production person could save on overall expenses in the long term*

# 6. Trim Costs and Findings

*Forgetting to include trims into a cost sheet will result in erosion of profits*

Whether it's zippers, labels, fusing, embroidery, elastic or other trims, make sure you are aware of the correct amount each garment needs. Haste makes waste and will take away your direct profit.

# 7. Contracting or Labor Costs

Sewing is another part of the garment cost that is usually 30% to 40% and should be fixed early in determining the cost of a garment.

Work only with reliable and legal contractors who can produce your goods on time.

*Note for California and New York apparel manufacturers – For your own records keep a copy of your contractors contracting license. Working with illegal contractors could result in confiscation of your goods, which could result in late deliveries or in some cases loss of a season. The contractor will also ask to see your manufacturing license and take a copy for their own records.*

# 8. The Cost of Cutting

Before cutting can begin make sure the fabric is checked on arrival for flaws and for width variations.

If you find irregularities with your fabrics Chargeback the mills as soon as possible. Timing is important.

Once you cut into the fabric, it is yours!

In-house cutting is often preferred to keep a check on waste.

Do not allow a build-up of aging fabric inventory.

# 9. Production Overheads

Real estate prices, electric costs, phone costs, accounting, transportation, quality control, shipping and packaging, even hangers and plastic bags are important expenses that should not be ignored.

# 10. Quality & Inventory Control

Quality control of the first production sample and production itself must have continuity otherwise there will be returns.

Important to make production samples for your contractor.

Returns equal reduction of your profits.

**Inventory Control**: Don't keep stock for more than a season. The longer you hang on to inventory the less it is worth.

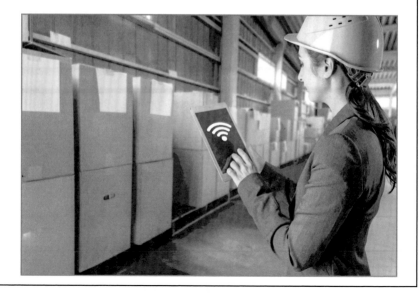

# Items Influencing Garment Cost

**If the garment cost is too high, then you must review the situation and find a solution to reducing the costs:**

$ Simplification of styling

$ Fabric yield

$ Total number of pattern pieces

$ Total number of notches

$ Total number of steps involved in the garment construction

$ Seam finishes, pressing, fusing, etc

If simplification cannot be achieved…

**DROP IT FROM THE LINE!!**

# Cost of Fabric

Consider buying directly from the mill (a problem for small companies, due to large minimums).

Can you afford a fabric rep?

Fabric shipping costs?

Number of yards per garment?

Ease of handling, silk, velvet, matching plaids, stretch, spreading needs, shrinkage under steam iron, pre-shrinking, etc.

Color variation, dye lots, garment dye, problems of fading in the store window, washing instructions, etc. It is important to test your own care labels. Swimwear manufacturers have to test garments for chloride and salt damage.

*Size of the cutting tickets or the units to be cut will also affect the final cost of the garment*

# Contracting Out Work

**Contracting work out to reliable contractors will allow you to keep your overhead expenses down. Some of the services you can contract:**

$ In-house, or outside sewing contractor

$ Grading & marker maker service

$ Cutting service

$ Inspection of finished goods

$ Picking and packaging orders

$ Shipping services

$ Accounting services

$ Payroll services

$ Domestic Production

$ Off-Shore Sourcing

*It is important to have references for any of the above contractors.*

# Construction Costs

$ Larger lots (contractors' costs go down when you have 300 garments or more)

$ Smaller businesses usually have to shop for contractors who specialize in smaller lots, which will increase unit cost

$ Grading and marking costs are computed on the number of the pattern pieces in one style

# Quality of Design

More complicated designs can be seen in "Better" priced clothing, along with more expensive quality fabrics, trims, linings, fusing and construction of garment.

A better fit and quality of garment should be evident in the higher-price range.

**Details of better fitting garment can be evident in** more seams, darts, inner construction and linings. Bigger seam allowances and hems equal more fabric usage, which in turn equals a more expensive garment.

**Examples of some seams:** French, flat felled, slot, topstitching, corded seams, open welt seams, more stitches per inch etc.

*Budget & Junior Clothing: Usually identified by cheaper construction, larger overlocked seams on the inside and less easy of fit in the garments*

# $tep Thirteen!

## Four Levels of Costing Methods

# Finally consider those four important costing methods

## Level 1 - Quickie Costing

Design department costing for the first sample

$ Estimate cost of each style before they are produced

$ Don't waste time and money to sample if they are obviously going to cost you out of your market niche

$ Quickie costing can be applied after a sample has been made and before they are added to the line

$ Pull the style before it gets into the line and will become a financial looser

# Level 2 - Costing for Sales

## Critical costing that must be exact

Management, Production, Design & Sales Dept. should all agree to your selling price.

$ This is where you set your selling price

$ You cannot change your wholesale price once it is set

$ All materials, cutting and contracting costs must be thoroughly understood and included

# Level 3 - Production Costing

Double check to see if your actual costs are correct. They should not be off by more than 3% to 5%.

This is where most problems can be found.

If costing is off you must cull the style.

If sales have been made, call buyer and tell them you have to pull the style but you have a **better** selling style for them. Never tell them you have made a mistake!

*Important to cut your losses when you know something is not working!*

# Level 4 - Account Dept. Costing

This is done at the end of the season to calculate average mark-up on all the garments sold and to track returns plus chargebacks.

Count every invoice and divide by sales, this will give you your season's average mark-up. Even better to do it by styles.

Accounting costing is done to help you to project sales and to understand how much cash flow you will need.

Lastly, the results of each style in either the line, or the collection provide historical information that will be important for both the following season and for the same season next year.

***Remember 80% of your business will be in 20% of your style***

# $tep Fourteen!

# Computer $oftware Needs

# Computer Software Programs to Calculate Your Costs and Help with Production Needs

**Once data is entered into one of the many apparel specific software programs an accurate costing is calculated for each style produced.**

$ Yardage cost

$ Labor costs

$ Fixed costs

$ Operational costs

$ These programs will calculate the gross profit margin and the net profit margins

*Important to remember, the computer is a tool and is only as good as the user, so be sure that the information programmed into the computer is correct! Check more than one software program to find the one which will suit your needs.*

# $tep Fifteen!

# Retail Math Costing

# Setting the Right Price

There are many outside influences that affect profitability and a retailer's bottom line. Setting the right price is a crucial step toward achieving that profit. Retailers are in business to make a profit, but figuring out what and how to price products may not come easily.

## Mark-up Pricing

**Markup on cost** can be calculated by adding a pre-set (often industry standard) profit margin, or percentage, to the cost of the merchandise.

**Markup on retail examples:** A t-shirt bought for $5 and sells for $10 has a mark-up of 100%. (Add $5 to the $5 cost to get the price.) A t-shirt bought for $2, which sells for $3, has a mark-up of 50%, (Add $1 to the $2 cost to get the price.)

Important that the retailer keeps the initial mark-up high enough to cover price reductions, discounts, shrinkage and other anticipated expenses, and still achieve a satisfactory profit. Retailers with a varied product selection can use different mark-ups on each product line.

**Retail discount pricing** and price reductions are a natural part of retailing. Discounting can include coupons, rebates, seasonal prices and other promotional markdowns.

**Markdowns:** Planned reduction in the selling price of an item, usually to take effect either within a certain number of days after seasonal merchandise is received or at a specific date.

Merchandise priced below cost is referred to as loss leaders. Although retailers make no profit on these discounted items, the hope is consumers will purchase other products at higher margins during their visit to the store.

Important to keep in mind for both the manufacturer and the retailer that the right product price is the price the consumer is willing to pay, while providing a profit to the retailer.

# Speed to Market

$ For the most part mass produced clothing is produced off-shore, but it is coming back!! Made in the USA is in demand.

$ Lower cost of off-shore workers wages has increased

$ Retailers are buying closer to selling – Demand for Speed to Market and Immediate

$ Smaller orders = good for new companies who are more nimble.

*In the long run this is good for cash flow*

# In Conclusion

Your wholesale price will often have nothing to do with the customers' perceived value of the garment. It relates to the final selling price, or the niche market that you have so carefully decided to fill.

Stay focused on your niche, control ALL your costs, and consistently monitor your business.

Listen to your customers' needs and your management team.

Find the right team to work with who understands the apparel business today! Even if you have to pay more to get the right people it will pay off in the long run.

It is important for a design driven company to find a good CPA who understands the apparel industry, and who can do your quarterly reports. Your factor will ask to see these reports and will use them to monitor how your company is running. Design and sales alone will not make a successful company. YOU NEED A GOOD CFO who will track your internal operations and your inventory to your sales.

Remember! It is not only about creating beautiful clothes, it is about running a profitable business; a commercial venture, from which you must realize a profit in order to stay in business.

# Appendices

# Retail Definitions

**80/20 Rule** - A commonly used rule of thumb, the 80/20 Rule, implies that a small number of events (20%) is responsible for a large percentage (80%) of the results.

**Alteration/Workroom Expense** - Expenses incurred when retailers make changes in their merchandise to satisfy special customer needs (e.g., clothing alterations or engravings). These are treated as part of the cost of goods sold.

**Average Inventory Cost** - Average inventory cost is found by adding the beginning cost inventory for each month plus the ending cost inventory for the last month in the period. If calculating for a season, divide by 7. If calculating for a year, divide by 13.

**Ad Slick** - Ad slicks refer to the final, camera-ready advertisement. It gets its name from the glossy paper on which it is printed.

**Acid-Test Ratio** - A measurement of how well a business can meet its short-term financial obligations without selling any inventory.

**Anchor Store** - A major retail store used to drive business to smaller retailers. These larger department stores or grocery stores are generally part of a retail chain and are the prominent business in a shopping mall.

**Big Box Stores** - Large stand-alone store with varying market niches.

**Bill of Lading** - A bill of lading is a document used as evidence that a transport company or carrier received goods from a shipper.

**Black Friday** - Black Friday is used to describe a number of historical Fridays in which an event led to public chaos or disaster.

**Booking Program** - A vendor booking program is the opportunity to view new products or samples now and to place an order for that merchandise to be delivered at a later date.

**Brand** - A brand is a name, symbol or other identifying mark for a seller's goods or services. It is distinct from other sellers.

**Brand Awareness** - A gauge of marketing effectiveness measured by the ability of a customer to recognize and/or recall a name, image or other mark associated with a particular brand.

**Break-Even Point** - What is the break-even point? The point in business where the sales equal the expenses. There is no profit and no loss.

**Brick and Mortar** - Brick and mortar store refers to retail shops that are located in a building as opposed to an online shopping destination, door-to-door sales, kiosk or other similar site not housed within a structure.

**Cash Discount** - Discounts granted to retailer for early payment of invoices.

**Cash Flow** - The movement of money in and out of a business and the resulting availability of cash.

**Category Killer** - A large retail chain store that is dominant in its product category. This type of store generally offers an extensive selection of merchandise at prices so low smaller stores cannot compete.

**Chain Store** - One of a number of retail stores under the same ownership and dealing in the same merchandise.

**Comp Sales** - What are comp sales? Comparable-store sales is a measurement of productivity in revenue used to compare sales of retail stores that have been open for a year or more. Historical sales data allows retailers to compare this year's sales in their store to the same period last year.

**Contribution Margin** - Contribution Margin is the difference between total sales revenue and total variable costs. The term is applied to a product line and is generally expressed as a percentage.

**Cost of Goods Sold (COGS)** - Includes the actual cost of the merchandise purchased plus freight charges and any alteration/workroom expenses. The amount of any cash discounts is subtracted.

**CRM - Customer Relationship Management** - Customer Relationship Management (CRM) is a business strategy designed to reduce costs and increase profitability by strengthening customer loyalty.

**Cyber Monday** - Cyber Monday is one of the busiest shopping days of the year for online retailers. Retailers notice a spike in sales on this day as many consumers who were too busy to shop over the Thanksgiving weekend or did not find what they were looking for, headed to the web on Monday from work or home to find bargains.

**Digital Signage** - Digital signage refers to a variety of technologies used to replace traditional retail signs. Instead of static print signs and billboards, digital signage is composed of electronic signs dispersing content and messages in the most targeted, interactive way.

**Drop Shipping** - Drop shipping is the process in which a retailer markets a product, collects payment from the customer and then orders the item from a supplier, to be shipped directly that customer. The retailer's profit is the difference between the amount collected and the amount spent. No inventory is held and the retailer is not involved in the shipping.

**EIN** - Employer Identification Number - An Employer Identification Number (EIN) is also known as a Federal Tax Identification Number, and is used to identify a business entity. Most businesses need an EIN. You may apply for an EIN in various ways, including online.

**Exit Interview** - Written or verbal conversation with a departing employee that show why the employee is leaving and how the business is viewed by others.

**Facing** - The number of identical products (or same SKU) facing out toward the customer. Facings are used in planograms and when zoning a retail store.

**Fair Trade** - Fair trade is an organized movement developed to promote standards of environmentalism and fair wages, alleviate global poverty and ensure that companies negotiate with the growers, manufacturers and producers of products for a fair price. This social-responsibility movement focuses on exports from developing countries.

**First In, First Out** - A method of stock rotation in which goods that are received first are sold first. Newly received product is stocked behind the older merchandise.

**FOB** - Shipping term used to indicate who is responsible for paying transportation charges.

**Gross Margin** - Sales revenue that remains after cost of goods sold has been deducted. It is the difference between what an item cost and for what it sells.

**Gross Margin Return On Investment** - A measure of inventory productivity that expresses the relationship between your total sales, the gross profit margin you earn on those sales, and the number of dollars you invest in inventory.

**Gross Sales** - The total of all sales made during any period of time.

**Hardlines** - A store department or product line primarily consisting of merchandise such as hardware, housewares, automotive, electronics, sporting goods, health and beauty aids or toys.

**Individual Markup** - The markup on one item of merchandise.

**Initial Markup** - The first markup placed on merchandise when it arrives in the store.

**Inventory** - Inventory is the merchandise a retail store has on-hand. The term also refers to the act of counting, itemizing and recording in-stock merchandise or supplies.

**Inventory Turnover** - The number of times during a given period that the average inventory on hand is sold and replaced.

**Journal** – A journal is the electronic or paper documentation of all transactions that have been recorded on a cash register.

**Keystone** - Keystone pricing is a method of marking merchandise for resell to an amount that is double the wholesale price + additional costs.

**Kiosk** - The term kiosk, as related to retailing, refers to a small stand-alone structure used as a point of purchase. This can be either a computer or display screen used to disseminate information to customers or may be a free-standing, full-service retail location. Kiosk are often found in malls and other high-traffic locations.

**Layaway** - Layaway is the act of taking a deposit to store merchandise for a customer to purchase at a later date.

**Loss Leader** - Merchandise sold below cost by a retailer in an effort to attract new customers or stimulate other profitable sales.

**Loss Prevention** - Loss prevention is the act of reducing the amount of theft and shrinkage within a business.

**Maintained Markup** – The markup that is actually realized after merchandise is sold.

**Markdown** - Reduction in the retail price of merchandise, usually to take effect either within a certain number of days after seasonal merchandise is received or at a specific date.

**Markdown Cancellation** - Increase in the retail price to offset all or any part of previously taken markdowns usually occurs when a markdown has been taken temporarily for promotional purposes.

**Marketing Calendar** - A marketing calendar is a tool used by retailers to show what marketing events, media campaigns and merchandising efforts are happening when and where, as well as the results.

**Markup** - The amount added to the cost of goods to determine the retail price.

**Markup Percentage** - The markup in dollars divided by either the retail price (markup based on retail) or the cost (markup based on cost).

**Merchandise Mix** - A merchandise mix is the breadth and depth of the products carried by retailers. Also known as product assortment.

**Minimum Advertised Price** - A suppliers pricing policy that does not permit its resellers to advertise prices below some specified amount. It can include the resellers retail price as well.

**Model Stock** - The desired merchandise assortment broken down according to the selection factors important to the store's customers.

**Mystery Shopping** - What is a mystery shopping program? Learn about this retailing term to effectively improve business.

**Net Sale** - Calculated by subtracting customer returns and allowance from gross sales.

**Odd-Even Pricing** - A form of psychological pricing that suggests buyers are more sensitive to certain ending digits.

**Off-Retail Percentage** - Calculated by dividing the dollar amount of markdown by the original retail price used primarily for advertising purposes.

**Open-to-Buy (OTB)** - The amount of money that the buyer has left to spend for a period.

**Operating Expenses** - All the expense incurred in operation a business both fixed and variable.

**Operating Statement** - A report that shows the profit or loss calculations for a store or department. Also called an income statement.

**Overbought** - A condition when buyers have purchased more than they planned during a specific period of time.

**Planned Purchases** - The dollar amount of merchandise a buyer plans to purchase during a period of time.

**Planogram** - Visual description, diagram or drawing of a store's layout to include placement of particular products and product categories.

**Point-of-Purchase Display** - Point-of-purchase displays, or POP displays, are marketing materials or advertising placed next to the merchandise it is promoting. These items are generally located at the checkout area or other location where the purchase decision is made. For example, The checkout counters of many convenience stores are cluttered with cigarette and candy POP displays.

**POS** - Point of Sale (POS) refers to the area of a store where customers can pay for their purchases. The term is normally used to describe systems that record financial transactions. This could be an electric cash register or an integrated computer system which records the data that comprises a business transaction for the sale of goods or services.

**Private Label** - Products which are generally manufactured or provided by one company under another company's brand.

**Product Breadth** - The product breadth is the variety of product lines offered by a retailer.

**Product Depth** - Product depth is the number of each item or particular style of a product on the shelves. Product depth is also known as product assortment or merchandise depth.

**Product Life Cycle** - The stages that a new product is believed to go through from the beginning to the end: Introduction, Growth, Maturity and Decline.

**Profit** - The amount of money remaining after operating expenses have been subtracted from gross margin.

**Profit Margin** - A ratio of profitability calculated as earnings divided by revenues. It measures how much out of every dollar of sales a retail business actually keeps in earnings.

**Product Life Cycle** - The stages that a new product is believed to go through from the beginning to the end: Introduction, Growth, Maturity and Decline.

**Purchase Order** - The contract between the buyer and the seller for the purchase of merchandise.

**Quantity Discount** - A reduction in price based on the amount purchased. May be offered in addition to any trade discount.

**Reductions** - Include markdowns, employee and consumer discounts, and inventory shortages.

**Retailing** - The sale of goods or commodities in small quantities directly to consumers.

**Returns and Allowances** - Include merchandise returned by customers or allowances granted to customers because of defective merchandise. Subtracted from gross sales to calculate net sales.

**Run of Paper** - Run of paper is an advertising term by newspapers referring to an advertisement that may be placed anywhere within the paper.

**Sales Floor** - The sales floor is the location of a retail store where goods are displayed and sales transactions take place. For example, the receiving of merchandise takes place in the stock room, but all direct sales and customer interactions are done on the sales floor.

**Shortages** - Merchandise disappearance due to shoplifting, employee theft, or paperwork errors.
**Shrinkage** - Retail shrinkage is a reduction or loss in inventory due to shoplifting, employee theft, paperwork errors and supplier fraud.

**Six-Month Merchandising Plan** - A tool used by retailers to translate profit objectives into a six-month framework for merchandise planning and control.

**SKU** - The Stock Keeping Unit (SKU) is a number assigned to a product by a retail store to identify the price, product options and manufacturer.

**Sliding** - A loss prevention term referring to the act of a cashier passing merchandise around the cash register barcode scanner without actually scanning the item.

**Softlines** - A store department or product line primarily consisting of merchandise such as clothing, footwear, jewelry, linens and towels.

**Standard Industrial Classification Code (SIC Codes)** - A coding system using four digits to identify specific industrial sectors within the Federal Government. The first two digits identify the broad industrial sector and the last two digits represent a facility's specialty within this broad sector.

**Staple Goods** - Staple goods are products purchased regularly and out of necessity. Traditionally, these items have fewer markdowns and lower profit margins. While price shifts may raise or lower demand for certain kinds of products, the demand for staple goods rarely changes when prices change.

**Standard Industrial Classification Code (SIC Codes)** - A coding system using four digits to identify specific industrial sectors within the Federal Government. The first two digits identify the broad industrial sector and the last two digits represent a facility's specialty within this broad sector.

**Stock-Sales Ratio Method** - A method of stock planning that involves maintaining inventory in a specific ratio to sales.

**Stock Turnover Rate** - Relates to the number of times the average stock is sold during a given period of time.

**Trade Discount - A discount on the list price given by a manufacturer** or wholesaler to a retailer.

**Trade Credit** - An open account with suppliers of goods and services.

**Triple Net Lease - NNN or Net-Net-Net** - A triple net lease is a rental agreement on a commercial property where the tenant agrees to pay all real estate taxes, building insurance, and maintenance on the property.

**Unit Assortment Plan** - Represents the merchandise buying plan as translated to specific pieces of merchandise (i.e., color, size or model).

**Visual Merchandising** - Visual merchandising is the art of implementing effective design ideas to increase store traffic and sales volume.

**Wholesale** - Wholesale is the sale of goods, generally in large quantity, to a retailer for resale purposes.

**Word-of-Mouth** - Possibly the most effective form of marketing. It is the verbal recommendation and positive approval by a satisfied customer.

**Working Capital** - Liquid assets available to build and grow a retail business. It is measured by current assets minus current liabilities. A positive working capital is needed until the shop can produce a profit.

# Apparel Acronyms

| | |
|---|---|
| ASN | ADVANCED SHIPPING NOTICE |
| BOM | BILL OF MATERIAL |
| C & F | COST AND FREIGHT |
| CAB | COMPUTER AIDED BUSINESS |
| CAD | CASH AGAINST DOCUMENTS |
| CAD | COMPUTER AIDED DESIGN |
| CAFTA | CENTRAL AMERICAN FREE TRADE AGREEMENT |
| CAM | COMPUTER AIDED MANUFACTURE |
| CFR | COST & FREIGHT |
| CFTA | CANADA FREE TRADE AGREEMENT |
| CIA | CASH IN ADVANCE |
| CIF | COST, INSURANCE, FREIGHT |
| CIM | COMPUTER INTEGRATED MANUFACTURING |
| CIT | COURT OF INTERNATIONAL TRADE |
| COD | CASH ON DELIVERY |
| COGS | COST OF GOODS SOLD |
| CPO | CUKSTOMER PURCHASE ORDER |
| CRM | CUSTOMER RELATIONSHIP MANAGEMENT |
| DBA | DOING BUSINESS AS |
| DLSE | DIVISION OF LABOR STANDARDS ENFORCEMENT |
| DOC | DEPARTMENT OF COMMERCE |
| DOS | DATA OPERATING SYSTEM |
| EDI | ELECTRONIC DATA INTERCHANGE |
| EIN | EMPLOYEE IDENTIFICATION NUMBER |
| EOM | END OF MONTH |
| FOB | FREE ON BOARD |
| FTC | FEDERAL TRADE COMMISSION |

| | |
|---|---|
| GUI | GRAPHICS USER INTERFACE |
| ITC | INTERNATIONAL TRADE COMMISSION |
| JPG | JPEG (Joint Photographic Experts Group) |
| L/C | LETTER OF CREDIT |
| LDP | LANDED-DUTY-PAID |
| NAFTA | NORTH AMERICAN FREE TRADE AGREEMENT |
| NRF | NATIONAL RETAIL FEDERATION |
| OTB | OPEN TO BUY |
| OTS | OPEN TO SELL |
| PDF | PORTABLE DOCUMENT FORMAT |
| PDS | PATTERN DESIGN SYSTEM |
| PO | PURCHASE ORDER |
| POP | POINT OF PURCHASE |
| POS | POINT OF SALE |
| PFD | PREPARE FOR DYE |
| RFID | RADIO FREQUENCY  IDENTIFICATION |
| RN# | REGISTERED NUMBER |
| ROI | RETURN OF INVESTMENT |
| SIC Code | STANDARD INDUSTRIAL CLASSIFICATION CODE |
| SKU | STOCK KEEPING UNIT |
| UCC | UNIFORMED CODE COUNCIL |
| UOM | UNIT OF MEASURE |
| UPC | UNIVERSAL PRODUCT CODE |
| UPS | UNITED PARCEL SERVICE |
| VAT | VALUE ADDED TAX |
| VPO | VENDOR PURCHASE ORDER |
| WIP | WORK IN PROCESS |
| WTO | WORLD TRADE ORGANIZATION |

# Fashion for Profit
# by Frances Ḥarder

The Fashion Business is a unique industry: artistic and creative, profit-driven and demanding. **Fashion for Profit** will take you to the heart of the business of fashion and give you the real facts.

A good idea and the right market niche can lead to your ultimate dream of running a successful apparel business. However, it is a multi-faceted industry with many important components that should be fully understood before taking that leap of faith. One missing link could mean failure. Knowledge is empowering and could save your savings! **Fashion for Profit** is the book that will support your ideas and help you to realize your dream. You will not only learn what you need to know, but what you want to know.

As you browse this 360-page plus book you will note that you will get more and more excited. Each chapter brings definitive information about each specific area of apparel manufacturing. You will find that many of the questions you thought would never be addressed anywhere are answered here in clear and understandable terms.

Frances Harder, designer, entrepreneur is also the founder of the LA based Fashion for Profit which provides much needed business intelligence, resources, and support to smaller and growing creative apparel companies.

Title: Fashion for Profit the book
Author: Frances Harder
Published: Newly revised 10th edition
Contact Information: Harder Publications
Tel: 310 541 7196
www.FashionForProfit.com
email: info@FashionForProfit.com
ISBN # 978-0-9727763-0-1
Retail: $49.99

# Brand Building for Profit
# "A Guide to Building a Brand"

From the author of Fashion for Profit and Costing for Profit, Brand Building For Profit by Frances Harder explains clearly and precisely what every apparel entrepreneur should consider when planning starting a new label. She also explains the many financial benefits of brand building.

In today brand conscious world, apparel companies such as Nike, Donna Karan, Patagonia, Levis and Calvin Klein have all become iconic American apparel labels that have influenced global popular culture.

Companies are ultimately recognized and identified by the name or logo they invent. A trademark can be the hottest asset a business owns because it distinguishes their product. Successfully branded labels lead to profitable licensing deals.

Brand Building for Profit examines the various steps a new company should take to begin this important brand-building process. A logo, trademark and a good story can lead to lucrative licensing opportunities—the goal of all new apparel manufacturers.

Additionally, creating a recognizable brand will also allow the manufacturer to demand a higher price for their product, because branded goods have a certain perceived value, often of consistent quality and fit. Interestingly, for the most part, branded products have no real added quality value that differentiates them from non-branded goods other than a branded logo.

When reading Brand Building for Profit, you will begin to understand the process of creating a brand, and the many possible branding opportunities that are available in today's global marketplace to apparel designers and manufacturers.

DETAILS:

Retail Price: $19.99

ISBN: 978-0-9727763-3-2

Author: Frances Harder

Series: 3rd Edition

Format/Binding: Perfect Paperback

Pages: 118

# Fashion for Profit – Forms For Profit
## CD – List of forms

Being prepared for doing business in a professional manner means using the correct forms and procedures common in the apparel industry. These forms will save valuable time in "getting it right"!

Forms For Profit gives you templates in which you can incorporate your logo, and samples to follow. The invoices, costing sheets and sales order forms have been built in a dynamic format so calculations can be achieved in Microsoft Excel. You also get Sales Order Form, Order Confirmation, Cutting Ticket, Bill of Materials, Pick Ticket, Purchase Orde Packing Slips Pattern Card, and Specification Sheets.

Also included are Sales Rep Agreement, Contractors Agreement, and Credit Check Application.

And, as a bonus, we've included professional body templates for womenswear, menswear and children's wear that can be used as a base for illustrations, and/or specifications. Print and use, or use as a guide in Illustrator software for design development.

Retail Price: $19.99
ISBN#: 978-0-9727763-8-7
Individual forms are also available for purchase for $5.00 each at www.FashionForProfit.com

# Fashion for Profit – Starting Your Own Apparel Business - (1 hour DVD)

The Fashion Business is a unique industry: artistic and creative, profit-driven and demanding. Fashion For Profit will take you to the heart of the business of fashion and give you the real facts. A good idea and the right market niche can lead to your ultimate dream of running a successful apparel business. However, it is a multi faceted industry with many important components that should be fully understood before taking that leap of faith. One missing link could mean failure. Knowledge is empowering and could save your savings! Fashion For Profit DVD will educate you and support your ideas to help you to realize your dream. You will not only learn what you need to know, but what you want to know. As you watch this one hour DVD you will note that you will get more and more excited. Frances explains each specific area of apparel manufacturing. You will find that many of the questions you thought would never be addressed anywhere are answered here in clear and understandable terms.

Retail Price: $19.99

ISBN#: 978-0-9845550-8-6

# Fashion for Profit Business Startup Package

Includes Fashion for Profit book & DVD, Costing for Profit book, Brand Building for Profit book, Forms for Profit CD, and a one hour seminar DVD on Fashion for Profit starting your own apparel business.

ISBN#: 978-0-9845550-9-3
Retail: $99.99
www.FashionForProfit.com

# Brand Building for Profit DVD by Frances Harder (1 hour)

In today's brand-conscious world, California apparel companies such as; Patagonia, Nike, Quiksilver, Levis and True Religion, have all become icons of American apparel labels, which have influenced global popular culture. The name or logo a company invents will ultimately be how they will be recognized and identified. Successfully branded labels lead to profitable licensing deals. This DVD seminar will examine the various steps a new company should take to begin the brand building process when entering the US market place, and the many US distribution channels.

Retail: $19.99

ISBN#: 978-0-9845550-5-5

# Fashion For Profit – Full size Basic Blocks

## NEW! $25.00 each block!

Basic Blocks to Make Your Own Patterns.

| | |
|---|---|
| Shirt blocks | Size 8 |
| Torso blocks | Size 8 |
| One dart bodice block | Size 8 |
| Two dart bodice block | Size 8 |
| Skirt block | Size 8 |
| Jacket blocks | Size 6 |
| Coat blocks | Size 8 |
| Bikini block | Size Medium |
| Pant block | Size 6 |
| Raglan block | Size 8 |

Go to **Fashionforprofit.com**
Download and print full size at Staples.
All sizes graded will soon be available for purchase from our website.

# Harder Publications Order Form

**Phone Orders:** (310) 541-7196
**Postal Orders:** Harder Publications
3402 Tanglewood Lane, Rolling Hills Estates, CA. 90274
**Internet Orders:** www.Fashionforprofit.com
**Email:** info@FashionForProfit.com

| Qty | Price* | Item |
|---|---|---|
|  | @$19.99 | Costing For Profit book |
|  | @$49.99 | Fashion For Profit book |
|  | @$19.99 | Brand Building For Profit Book |
|  | @$19.99 | Forms For Profit CD |
|  | @$99.99 | Business Starter Package – Costing For Profit, Fashion For Profit book & DVD, Brand Building for Profit, DVD Starting your Own Apparel Business and CD Forms for Profit |
|  | @$19.99 | Brand Building for Profit DVD |

*Plus tax, shipping and handling
** Online videos can be purchased at **www.fashionforprofit.com**
**Teaching guide and PowerPoint presentation available for instructional use on college orders.**

Please add 9.75% for products shipped to California addresses.
**Shipping:** $8 US / $20 International for the first item and $5 for each additional item.

Name: _____

Address:_____

City:_____ State: ____ Zip: _____

Phone: _____ Country: _____

Email Address: _____

**Payment Type:**
❏ Check enclosed payable to: Harder Publications
❏ Credit Card    ❏ Visa    ❏ MasterCard    ❏ PayPal
Credit card #: _____

Name on card: _____ Exp date: _____

**Please send more information on:**
❏ Seminars   ❏ Consulting   ❏ Teaching Material